Totally AMAZING FACTS ABOUT CREEPY-CRAWLIES

PENELOPE NELSON

raintree
a Capstone company — publishers for children

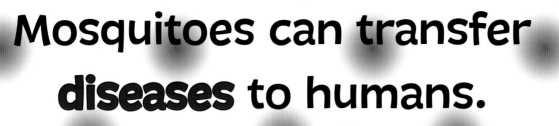

Mosquitoes can transfer **diseases** to humans.

A mosquito larva is sometimes called a "wiggler".

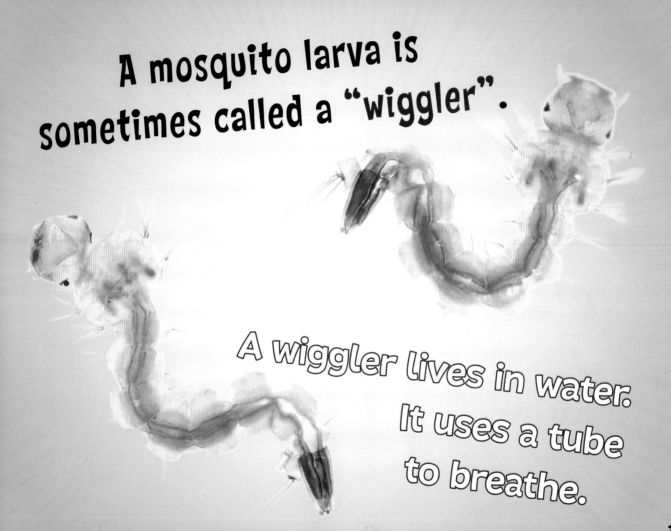

A wiggler lives in water. It uses a tube to breathe.

Once they are in human hair, head lice drink blood from the scalp.

The wing tips of Atlas moths look like SNAKE heads!

The dead leaf **butterfly** looks like a **dead leaf.**

Predators are less likely to eat me!

Is that bird poo?

No, it's a **GIANT** swallowtail caterpillar!

The legs of an orchid mantis look like flower petals.

A dragonfly has two pairs of wings that can beat separately.

It can fly at 32 kilometres (20 miles) per hour!

DRAGONFLIES have been around for **300 MILLION YEARS!**

A **DRAGONFLY'S** eyes make up almost all of its head. Large eyes help the **DRAGONFLY** catch prey.

Dragonfly larvae

DRAGONFLIES can stay in their larval stage for up to two years.

A dragonfly breaks through its larval skin.

spine

A saturniid caterpillar's spines
can sting attackers.

tongue

A hummingbird moth's tongue is longer than its whole body!

Caterpillars can feel through the hairs on their bodies.

Moths get ready to fly by vibrating their wings.

A luna moth's tail spins behind it as it flies.

As a luna moth flies, its tail makes noise. It sounds like **WINGBEATS!**

The noise confuses bats that are hunting the luna moth.

Some cockroaches hatch from eggs inside their mother's body.

Surinam toads hatch out of holes in their mother's back.

The Australian blue ant isn't really an ant.
It's a flower wasp.

Australian blue ants will sting a mole cricket. Then the blue ants lay their EGGS inside the cricket.

After hatching, the young blue ants eat the paralysed CRICKET!

The giant weta is the **HEAVIEST** insect in the world.

It can weigh as much as
THREE MICE!

Antarctica is the only continent that does not have spiders.

Jumping spiders can leap up to **50 TIMES** their body length!

Tarantulas live underground. Their burrows are lined with **WEBS**.

Their large fangs inject venom into prey.

fangs

A tarantula **SUCKS** out the prey's insides.

The Goliath birdeater spider can grow to be **30.5 CENTIMETRES** (1 foot) long.

This spider has been known to eat **BIRDS**. It will also eat small **MICE** or **LIZARDS**!

Its fangs are nearly 2.5 centimetres (1 inch) long.

Even though spiders have eight eyes, some can't see very well.

Spiders don't like the smell of peppermint.

All spiders make **SILK**, but some don't spin webs.

A black widow spider's venom is more **TOXIC** than a rattlesnake's venom!

But a spider injects less venom, so it's not as deadly.

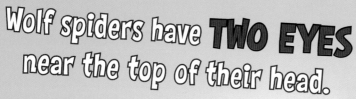
Wolf spiders have **TWO EYES** near the top of their head.

A wolf spider has eight eyes lined up in three rows.

Wolf spiders lay several DOZEN EGGS at once. The mother will carry the eggs on her back.

Assassin bugs are sneaky!
They will wait and
trap their prey.

An assassin bug
sucks out its prey's
body fluids through a
straw-like mouthpart.

An assassin bug uses dead bugs as camouflage. It glues the dead bugs on its back like a suit of armour.

An assassin bug can carry 20 dead ants on its back at a time.

Grasshoppers living in cities chirp louder than country grasshoppers.

CICADAS are so loud that humans can hear them from 0.8 kilometres (½ mile) away.

A froghopper bug is just 6 millimetres (0.2 inches) long. It can jump more than 0.6 metres (2 feet) into the air.

A pygmy mole cricket can jump more than 280 times its own body length!

If dung beetles didn't exist, most of the ground would be covered in

POO!

A dung beetle can carry more than

1,000 TIMES

its own weight.

Some researchers think dung beetles may use stars in the night sky as a navigation system.

Male stag beetles are **battle beetles!** They have antler-shaped jaws for **fighting.**

A male giraffe weevil uses its **LONG NECK** to fight.

My neck may be long, but it's not as long as a giraffe's neck!

49

Bombardier beetles spray attackers with chemicals.

The spray can
get as **HOT** as
100 degrees Celsius
(212 degrees Fahrenheit)!

Some ladybirds have **STRIPES** instead of **DOTS**.

I don't look weird – I just have a different style.

Cramer's 88 butterfly has the number 88 on its wings.

Some beetles have curved ANTENNAE for smelling.

antennae

Something smells good!

SUNBURST
diving beetles can breathe underwater.

A **TORTOISE BEETLE** hides its legs and head under its shell when attacked.

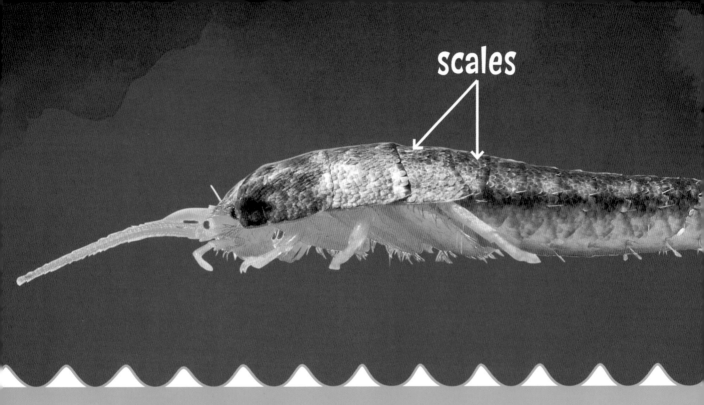

scales

A **silverfish** isn't actually a fish. But this insect does have **scales**.

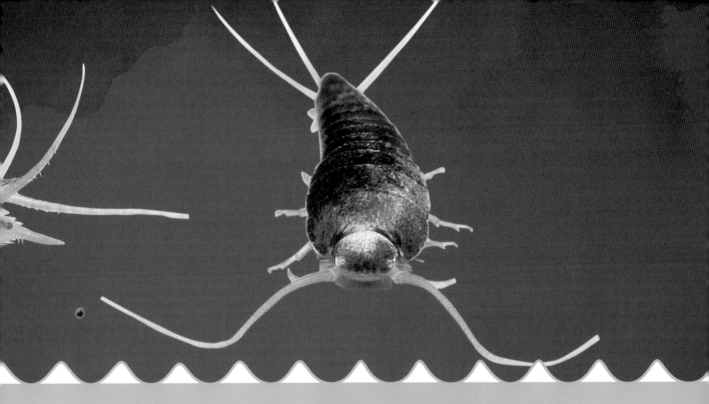

The scales are slippery and help the insect escape predators.

BED BUGS find sleeping humans by sensing the carbon dioxide humans exhale.

58

A bed bug can attack a person more than **400 TIMES** in one night!

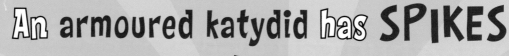

An armoured katydid has **SPIKES** on its body. The spikes scare off predators.

spikes

Armoured ground crickets will eat plants, insects and even birds!

62

Fleas will nest on furry hosts, such as dogs and cats.

Fleas drink the blood of their host!

A female flea can lay up to 50 eggs each day.

The biggest scorpion
is almost
18 centimetres
(7 inches) long!

Scorpions use their **POISONOUS TAILS** to kill or paralyse prey!

The **LONGEST INSECT** ever found was a stick insect. It was almost 56 centimetres (22 inches) long!

STICK INSECTS change their colour to match their surroundings.

When a queen bee dies, the worker bees feed young female bee larvae a special food. The food is called **ROYAL JELLY**.

The first fertile bee to hatch will kill the other female bee larvae. She will then become the **QUEEN** bee.

Bees talk to each other by **dancing**.

This dance tells other bees where flowers are located.

I've been practising all day!

Scientists call it the "Waggle Dance".

A jewel wasp stings a cockroach's brain. Then the wasp tricks the cockroach into being food for its babies.

Jewel wasp

A tick can grow to be as big as a marble.

When a tick finds an animal, it inserts a tube into the animal's skin and sucks up blood.

claws

Centipedes use their POISONOUS claws to paralyse prey!

Millipedes can have more than 300 pairs of legs.

Is that a tree?
No, it's a Christmas tree worm!

Their **EYES** are hidden inside their gills.

gills

Bobbit worms can grow up to **3 METRES** (10 feet) long!

A slug can have up to 100,000 teeth.

A slug's slime helps it slither smoothly over the ground.

A female slug can reproduce without a mate.

Maggots eat rotting meat.

Maggots are fly larvae!

Maggots can help solve crimes. Scientists study maggots on corpses to determine a time of DEATH.

Earthworms can regrow lost body parts.

The longest earthworm found was 41 centimetres (16 inches) long.

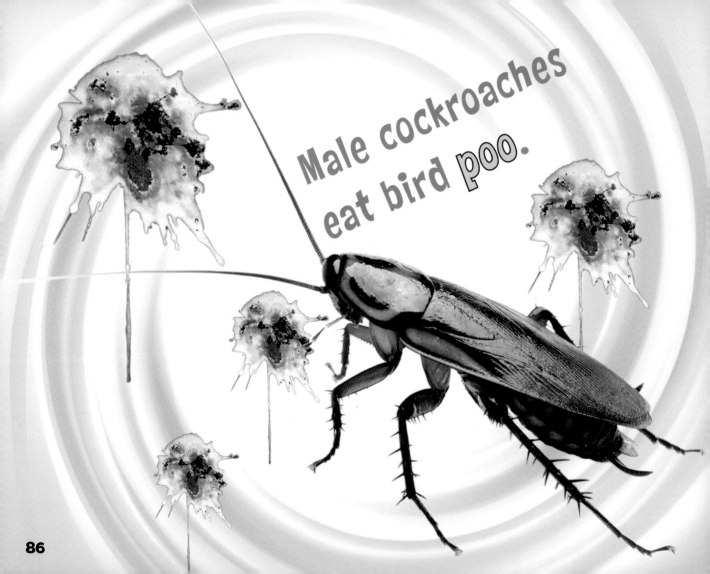

Male cockroaches eat bird poo.

A **COCKROACH** can live for
a week without its head.
It will die only because it can't
eat or drink without its head.

A scorpionfly flies away with its prey.

Male scorpionflies give "GIFTS" to females.

The presents are DEAD BUGS!

Earwigs sometimes eat their young.

If a mother scorpion can't find enough insects to eat, she will eat her BABIES.

A praying mantis moves so **QUICKLY**, a human eye can't see it catch a bug.

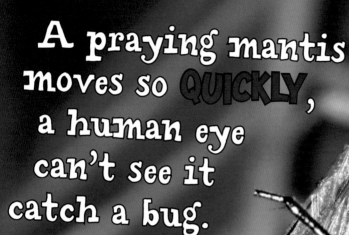

Praying mantises usually eat other bugs **HEADFIRST**.

A female praying mantis sometimes **EATS A MALE** praying mantis.

isopod

Some isopods eat the tongues of fish.

A young ant eats its parent's **SICK**.

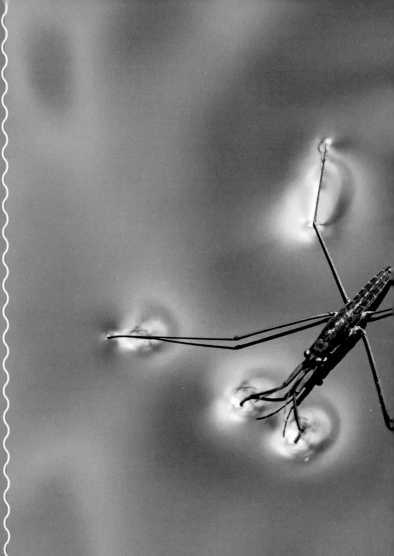

Water striders,
a type of
water bug,
have tiny hairs
on their legs.
The hairs help
them to glide
on water.

Coconut crabs have strong **pincers**. They can crack coconut shells!

Crabs talk to each other by waving their pincers!

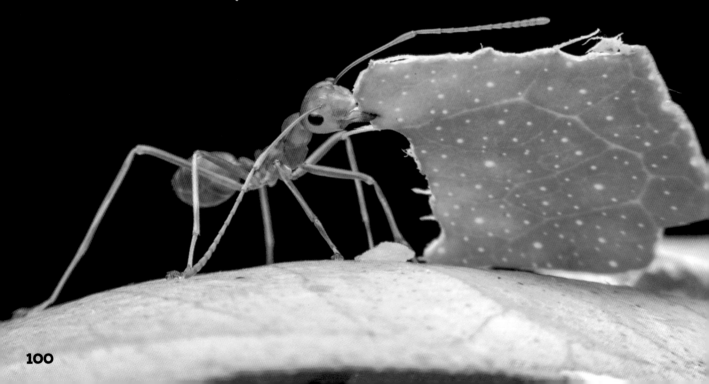

The jaws of a leaf cutter ant vibrate 1,000 TIMES per second!

Leaf cutter ants work together in groups of hundreds or thousands.

Fire ants latch onto each other and swim together to survive during a flood.

Driver ants communicate with their antennae.

Saharan silver ants can live in **49°C** (120°F) heat. They use their **HAIR** to reflect sunlight and control body temperature.

Ants cross gaps in leaves and rocks by using other ants as **BRIDGES.**

Termites can unearth **GOLD** when building their nests.

Termite mounds can be up to 6 metres (20 feet) high!

Termites line their homes with their own POO!

GLOSSARY

burrow   hole or tunnel used as a house

carbon dioxide   colourless, odourless gas produced by the act of breathing

fangs   long pointed teeth

gill   body part that some insects use to breathe underwater

larva   insect that is not fully developed

navigation system   way of finding out one's position

predator   animal or insect that hunts other animals for food

prey   animal that is hunted by another animal for food

reproduce   create offspring

toxic   poisonous

unearth   find something in the ground through digging

venom   poisonous liquid used by some insects, reptiles and arachnids when they bite or sting

FIND OUT MORE

BOOKS

Ants, Lucy Bowman (Usborne, 2016)

Crazy Creepy Crawlies (Extreme Animals), Isabel Thomas (Raintree, 2013)

It's All About Beastly Bugs (Kingfisher, 2015)

WEBSITES

www.dkfindout.com/uk/animals-and-nature/insects/what-is-an-insect
Find out more about insects on this website.

www.scienceprojectideas.co.uk/facts-about-insects-minibeasts.html
Read fun facts about insects and minibeasts.

INDEX

111

Raintree is an imprint of Capstone Global Library Limited, a company incorporated in England and Wales having its registered office at 264 Banbury Road, Oxford, OX2 7DY – Registered company number: 6695582

www.raintree.co.uk
myorders@raintree.co.uk

Text © Capstone Global Library Limited 2018

Edited by Alyssa Krekelberg
Designed by Kazuko Collins
Original illustrations © Capstone Global Library Ltd 2018
Picture research by Alyssa Krekelberg
Production by Laura Polzin and Kazuko Collins
Printed and bound in China.

ISBN 978 1 4747 4290 0
21 20 19 18 17
10 9 8 7 6 5 4 3 2 1

British Library Cataloguing in Publication Data
A full catalogue record for this book is available from the British Library.

Acknowledgements
We would like to thank the following for permission to reproduce photographs:
Alamy: blickwinkel, 45, Francisco Martinez-Clavel Martinez, 53, GFC Collection, 14, Graphic Science, 22, Mike Veitch, 94, Nature Picture Library, 49, 65, NSP-RF, 61, Redmond O. Durrell, 103, WaterFrame, 79; iStockphoto: 2ndLookGraphics, 86 (bird poop), GoodGnom, 42–43 (music notes), javier29, 109, LCPhoto66, 27, Prikhnenko, 28–29 (spiderwebs), ranplett, cover (bottom right), voinSveta, 102 (life raft); National Geographic: James P. Blair, 50–51; Science Source: Dr Morley Read, 20, Emanuele Biggi/FLPA, 73, Francesco Tomasinelli, 93, Louise Murray, 24, Nature's Images, 55 (right), Tom McHugh, 21; Shutterstock Images: 2happy, cover (top right), aaltair, 10–11, Amanda Nicholls, 78, Andrea Mangoni, 29, Andrey Pavlov, 95, apiguide, 54, asawinimages, 28 (right), Audrey Snider-Bell, 30 (top), 31, AVprophoto, 108 (foreground), bearacreative, 7 (right), BeeRu, 71, Brian Lasenby, 66, Butterfly Hunter, 17, Cathy Keifer, 33 (left), chakkrachai nicharat, cover (top left), Charly Morlock, 64, Christian Musat, 13 (right), 38, Cornel Constantin, 32 (left), Cosmin Manci, 63, CPM PHOTO, 42, Dancestrokes, 70 (right), Dario Lo Presti, 83, devil79sd, 5 (foreground), Dr Morley Read, 92, 102, Eric Isselee, cover (bottom left), EW CHEE GUAN, 3, Ezume Images, 77 (top), Fauzan Maududdin, 70 (left), Francmasc, 67, george photo cm, 16 (bottom), goldenjack, 48, GUDKOV ANDREY, 99, Gyvafoto, 30 (bottom), Helen Sushitskaya, 62, Hendroh, 55 (left), Henrik Larsson, 37, 90, Huaykwang, 52, IanRedding, 44, Igor Cheri, 18 (top), Ilin Sergey, 24–25, Irina Kozorog, 72, jack_photo, 101, Jan Miko, 96–97, JasonYoder, 18 (bottom), john michael evan potter, 46, Jurik Peter, 56–57, kamnuan, 82, Katoosha, 28 (left), khlungcenter, 100, kim7, 106–107, kurt_G, 41–40, Kutikan, 108 (background), KYTan, 98 (left), 98 (right), L Falbraith, 60, LHF Graphics, 33 (peppermints), Lightspring, 58, Lindarks, 47 (telescope), Lindwa, 26, Littlekidmoment, 4, Matt Jeppson, 19, Melinda Fawver, 74–75 (ticks), 75 (left tick), Mirko Graul, 68–69, Moriah-Diamond, 81, Natasha_S, 9 (right), PaleBlue, 16 (top), Paul Looyen, 36, Pavel Krasensky, 59, 91, 104–105, pbombaert, 74–75 (marbles), Petrov Anton, 88–89, PongMoji, 2, Protasov AN, 5 (background), QiuJu Song, 13 (left), Rostislav Kralik, 15, Sari Oneal, 34–35, sarocha wangdee, 76, Sebastian Janicki, 9 (left), 32 (right), seeyou, 86 (cockroach), Soyka, 12 (left), Srunyu Poonyaphitak, 87, Starover Sibiriak, 12 (right), Steve Byland, 43, Szasz-Fabian Jozsef, 25, 80, Tanita_B, 33 (right), Teim, 77 (bottom), Thawornnurak, 7 (left), Tyler Fox, 8 (top), 8 (bottom), Vitalii Hulai, 47 (dung beetle), warmer, 84, wawritto, 85, WeStudio, 6, xpixel, 23 (bottom), Zablotsky, 23 (top)

Design Elements: Red Line Editorial, Shutterstock Images, and iStockphoto

Every effort has been made to contact copyright holders of material reproduced in this book. Any omissions will be rectified in subsequent printings if notice is given to the publisher.

All the internet addresses (URLs) given in this book were valid at the time of going to press. However, due to the dynamic nature of the internet, some addresses may have changed, or sites may have changed or ceased to exist since publication. While the author and publisher regret any inconvenience this may cause readers, no responsibility for any such changes can be accepted by either the author or the publisher.